THIS MELLOW WORLD

Portuguese-Americans and Contemporary Civic Culture in Massachusetts
Edited by Clyde W. Barrow

Through a Portagee Gate
Charles Reis Felix

In Pursuit of Their Dreams: A History of Azorean Immigration to the United States
Jerry R. Williams

Sixty Acres and a Barn
Alfred Lewis

Da Gama, Cary Grant, and the Election of 1934
Charles Reis Felix

Distant Music
Julian Silva

Representations of the Portuguese in American Literature
Reinaldo Silva

The Holyoke
Frank X. Gaspar

Two Portuguese-American Plays
Paulo A. Pereira and Patricia A. Thomas
Edited by Patricia A. Thomas

Happy People in Tears
João de Melo
Preface by Onésimo T. Almeida
Translated by Elizabeth Lowe with Deolinda Adão

Return Flights
Jarita Davis
Foreword by Christopher Larkosh

Behind the Stars, More Stars: The Tagus/Disquiet Collection of Luso-American Writing
Edited by Christopher Larkosh and Oona Patrick

The Poems of Renata Ferreira
Edited by Frank X. Gaspar

News on the American Dream: A History of the Portuguese Press in the United States
Alberto Pena Rodríguez
Preface by Frank F. Sousa
Translated by Serena Rivera with Gloria de Sá

Leaving Pico
REVISED EDITION
Frank X. Gaspar
Foreword by Antonio Ladeira

The Undiscovered Island
REVISED EDITION
Darrell Kastin
Introduction by Katharine Vaz

Migration, Mill Work, and Portuguese Communities in New England
Edited by Cristiana Bastos, Bela Feldman-Bianco, and Miguel Moniz

THIS MELLOW WORLD

RAYMOND OLIVER

TAGUS PRESS
University of Massachusetts Dartmouth
North Dartmouth, MA

Tagus Press is the publishing arm of the Center for Portuguese Studies and Culture at the University of Massachusetts Dartmouth.
Center director: Anna M. Klobucka

Portuguese in the Americas 31
Tagus Press at the University of Massachusetts Dartmouth
© 2025 Raymond Oliver

Executive Editor: Mario Pereira
Series Editor: Francisco Cota Fagundes
Copyedited by: Dawn Potter
Cover by: Frank Gutbrod
Designed and typeset by: Jen Jackowitz

For all inquiries, please contact:
Tagus Press Center for Portuguese Studies and Culture
University of Massachusetts Dartmouth
285 Old Westport Road
North Dartmouth, MA 02747–2300
(508) 999-8255, fax (508) 999-9272
https://www.umassd.edu/portuguese-studies-center/

ISBN: 978-1-951470-21-0
Library of Congress control number: 2025933403

For my family, present and disappeared

CONTENTS

HOMAGE TO GONÇALO MENDES

PREFACE

I never met my grandfather, António Raimundo de Oliveira, but his widow was my first babysitter. She never learned English, really, so I like to think I was imprinted by my grandmother's Portuguese the way a duck is said to be imprinted by whomever it first sees upon leaving the egg—its mother, a human, a turkey—to the point of following that creature around forever after. The analogy is suspect, of course, because my Yankee mother came first; but as it happens I've been following Vovó all my life, as a matter of conscious yet fated choice, in my need— variously intense—to possess Portuguese. So I think Vovó talked to me a great deal, saying in many different ways: "Come here."

My grandparents both came to Boston in 1900 from the Azores, from the part of São Miguel called Bretanha, bringing along several children. My father was born in this country, but his first language was Portuguese, and I heard it now and then, though he didn't teach it to me except in little phrases and words. He was a difficult man, highly talented, not formally educated (he quit school at fifteen), and pursued by many demons, especially alcohol. Because this powerful, vivid person, very hard on me, was Portuguese, everything I came to associate with "Portuguese" was deeply colored by my sense of him and his exotic-seeming family. It was both intimate and alien—a strong mixed drink of delicious, ironic earthiness, darkly frightening anxieties, and fate, *fado*; and I have been trying since childhood not merely to tolerate that drink but to like it. I ended up loving it.

My lifelong obsession with these matters led finally, almost inevitably, to visiting São Miguel, where my wife Mary Anne and I spent the month of May 1989. I had to experience directly where this obsession had begun. The visit provided something like a multidimensional, multisensual vocabulary of things Azorean. But it took a book, the last work of Portugal's most famous novelist, to frame and focus for me the Matter of Portugal.

I had taught myself the language, sporadically, so I was ready when, after many years, I came upon that marvelous novel by Eça de Queiroz, *A Ilustre Casa de Ramires* (1900), *The Illustrious House of Ramires*. I had never in all my reading met anyone like Gonçalo Mendes Ramires, who exactly, triumphantly, reconciles elements that I had found incompatible: he is at the same time very attractive in ways I most appreciate, very similar to myself in certain respects that may or may not be attractive, and he is eminently Portuguese. It remained only to speak with Gonçalo and pay him homage, especially in two ways I like to think that he, in turn, would much appreciate. He is a very formal gentleman, quite precise in his manners, dress, and language, so I wrote this book almost wholly in strictly formal verse, sometimes with end rhyme or half-rhyme, and often in blank verse, where each line is bound together by assonance or full rhyme. The second main tribute I've paid him is imitation. Throughout the novel, he is shown struggling with a novel of his own about his distinguished family, older than the kingdom. At some point he finds an obscure book published fifty years earlier by his uncle, Tio Duarte; it is an epic poem about the illustrious Ramires family. So, of course, Gonçalo happily ransacks it for materials and inspiration— rewording, paraphrasing, alluding, commenting, interpreting; in a word, plagiarizing. (But plagiarism, says the great Viennese poet von Hofmannsthal, "is a matter of taste.") In similar ways, I have made use of the Gonçalo story as an elaborate gloss on my own family and that month-long visit to the Azores.

The title of this book comes from the last two lines of its last page.

ACKNOWLEDGMENTS

Many of these poems were previously published in *Gávea-Brown, Prairie Schooner,* and the *Southern Review.* I am grateful to their editors.

THIS MELLOW WORLD

Portuguese

This is no tongue to turn a compliment,
Or twist a curse too graceful to resent,
Or speak in flames grandly of heaven and hell;
Its sound is intimate, like the frying-smell
Of garlic. With liquids like a heavy wine,
It speaks of sweet-loaves, olives packed in brine,
Chestnuts and squash; its consonants are blurred,
Nasals insinuating, diphthongs slurred
With overtones, like some ignoble wish;
It is a language of linguiça, fish,
Mary, and Christ—staples on which to fatten
Both flesh and soul. Among the sons of Latin,
It seems a country cousin richly crude;
Yet one must praise a tongue that savors food
And God with gusto: familial Portuguese,
In whose irregular moods I feel at ease.

FAMILY

Vovó

I saw her last foreshortened in her coffin,
Propped like a puppet in a little box,
The rigid insult—silent stillness—of death
Compounded by this extra lessening
To toylike nothing, husk of has-been flesh.
Formerly, she'd been merely short and shapeless,
Thanks to her fat and twenty years of black—
Bandanna, shawl, and dress enfolding all
But pallid toothless blue-eyed smiling face,
Cheery indifference of the aged widow.
(Of all the things she said, I just recall
Three words—"Raymond, come here!," "Rámon, vem cá!,"
Which I could never do, except to hug her.)

I see in early photos contoured cheekbones,
A sculptured face with teeth to shape her jaw:
Beautiful as her name, Francisca, née
Tavares. Earlier, before the voyage
To Boston, nineteen-hundred, when she lost
Her land and language, she had had a future
At first as common as the fresh-turned earth,
Girl of Pilar, Bretanha, São Miguel,
Açores, Portugal—the sort of *fado*
Sung to her peasant sort for centuries:
A husband good for children, little wealth,
And tearful strife between his wine and work;
Sunday church becoming daily with age.

But Chica found António, whom the priest
Had taught to read, whose writing like engraving
Amazed the letterless and promised greatness,
And who would take her past the common fate
With strength and handsomeness and brains, and did.

Earlier, little girl now wholly lost
(Except I've heard her cottage floor was dirt),
She played in honest light and air, the eighteen-
Seventies in Pilar, which came and went
As slowly, quickly, finally as time
Will do, like yours, like mine; leaving her childhood
Forever in the freedom of forgetting,
Unlike that propped-up husk I can't forget.

Photo of Bretanha,
São Miguel, Açores, 1870–1889

Brushy dishevelment
of bushes and trees crowding
the wide low hill of background,
their insistent green
to be inferred from the blacks and
greys of the photo—
but foreground is five
people, all dressed all in white
with thatched-roof cottage on right,
its wall of wildly irregular stones and
thin black doorway as high as the wall,
with profiled woman in it; then sitting
boy, his head merging
in size and color with the stones; then
lovely-faced sitting teenage girl, maybe
working at bench; then tiny girl,
arms raised in diamond-shape
to frame her face;
then like an afterthought
a standing boy at a distance
beholding the camera.

That nineteenth-century instant, snapped
and snatched from oblivion
right there,
was almost certainly not preserved
elsewhere.

I like to think unprovably but
conceivably
that these were my family, as
minutely alive as I.

Words for António
Raimundo de Oliveira

Your name, like Baudelaire's grand albatross,
Could not survive out of its element,
And part of you did not survive its loss.

The change to "Tony Oliver" had rent
Your past from present, half from half, with shocks
That, shifting your articulation, bent

Both tongue and back. From warm volcanic rocks
Lush in the North Atlantic, you had come:
St. Michael's, Azores—Islands of the Hawks.

Did the defending angel hover, dumb,
As you heaved barrels on the Boston docks?

Vovô's Tale of the Old Days

Fierce with purpose though sick, he made his way
Near midnight to his enemy's fresh grave,
Up on the hilltop where the wind was cold;
And not to pray for Zé Machado's soul,
In final Christian willingness to forgive him,
But to revile him with a fury driven
By hatred, shaped by old intimacy.
At last, though cursing made him weak, he seized
His sword in both his hands and drove it down,
Deep in the dark, into the swelling mound
Below the head of the grave. But as he turned
To leave, he couldn't: with a sudden, firm
Jolt, he was held around the throat and from
Behind. The tremor seized his heart.
                              Undone
By terror he died, not noticing his cloak—
Nailed to the ground by his avenging stroke.

Visiting Aunt Mamie's House

It was a different Sunday dullness there,
The kitchen spread with newspapers to spare
The wax protecting the linoleum
That covered boards and beams that kept us from
The cellar set on dirt—of which the floors
Were made, in houses in the poor Azores,
Our family place. Such messy indirection,
To keep a glossy surface! as protection
Against the deep remembered dirt.
                                    But dull:
Papers as carpet; radio to mull
The grownup voices (droning cut by yells)
With Sunday music-syrup that sometimes swells
To overflow; the oily, salty food;
The rattling Portuguese. It set my mood
Immovably, as if in solid fat.
Family? I have nothing to do with that—
Neither with 'Shlash'ca,* smiling wordless crone,
Assigned so girls would never be alone,
Duenna-scarecrow, shriveler of men;
Nor Rosie evil-eye; not even when
My uncles—Tony, Frank, and Manuel—
Inscribed the heavens with a little hell-
Fire, *foguetes*, "forgets," the Fourth of July.

---

* This is how the name Escolástica sounded to the poet.

They twinkle now, distant in the mind's eye;
But then how dull they were. That was my name
For incomprehension, self-exclusion, shame.

RJO, 1910–1982

For Christmas plays they made you Baby Jesus,
You were so fair. It couldn't have been easy,
Once you had understood who you had been.
And you especially pleased your father, since
You spoke the purest Portuguese of all,
The kind Jesus would speak, without a fault.
But you were a ghetto urchin in New England,
Where the sirens of the ideal were singing . . .
Not in a Latin language, nor of That Baby,
Nor in churches of the Five Wounds, Our Lady
Of Sorrows or Pilar, or the Good Death;
They sang of Anglo beauty and success.
You listened. Justified by work, like Anglos,
Chastely correct though vivid with your language,
Now English, marrying a sumptuous redhead—
As Yankee as a pot of beans, as steady
As Plymouth Rock—you made yourself a salesman
Of drugs, not fearing God or man but failure.
(Drugs are like words, a way of making sickness
Or pain—so easily, by mouth—diminish.)

You climbed up toward success, by dressing sharp
And always being bright, hitting your mark
With words. But whisky was the juice that ran
Your Yankee high-wire act, and it had planned
Your future differently. You drank, she ate,
Until your tension and your redhead's shape—

Working together, step by step—had swollen,
The one breaking, the other overflowing.
And as my mother happily fattened, turning
More indolent of mind, your pride was hurting
("My wife the *pata-choca!*") like open sores
That all could see, and so you drank some more,
And lost the Upjohn job, and turned from people,
A Latin malcontent, sarcastic, wreaking
Verbal wreckage on many, often women,
But mostly me. I looked like her. I didn't
Play baseball. (There's a snapshot from the beach,
Showing you with a baseball, hand on knee,
A shark-wide smile, ready to lob it maybe
A yard at the tiny boy who stood there vaguely
Shouldering bat like rifle, staring at
The camera, held by mother.)
                              You weren't "Dad,"
"Father"; I had no name for you, not face
To face. It would have been too intimate;
Those tender nerves had died.
                              I disappointed;
You were a troll with whom I was acquainted,
Something whose habits must be learned, and moods
Foreseen, so I could make the counter-move.
At last, a virtuoso of withdrawal,
I no more felt my anger, fear, or sorrow,
Than I could feel for you. Or for your language
And all it meant, as mute now as my anguish.

The Ruby Dye

They seemed to yell or mumble Portuguese,
Never to speak—since anyone who speaks,
I understand. Their words were no less strange
Than *caldo* or *linguiça* that I strained
To eat, or banging, flashing fireworks
I tried to like, or hugs in lieu of words
From bread-soft Vovo, or the frightening shape
Of Joe Medeiros's head. "Anglo is safe,
Latin disturbing," as my little self,
In all but words, did not quite think but felt:
A noisiness of garlic, squishy smells
Of language, crimson dancing—things to squelch
The hope of this unsettled child to keep
His life a well-set table, clean and neat.
I needed that. My father, drunk at table,
Stormy as the Azores with rage or hatred,
Scorned me as if he'd caught me eating spaghetti
With bare hands and wiping my nose with lettuce.
Denounced by him, the Portuguese, my squalor
Was somehow Portuguese as well, and horrid:
Birthright of stinking, slippery fishiness,
Of failure ignominious and grotesque.
So visiting his family made me shrink
Into a self where (would-be!) alien stinks,
More and more, disturbed me. Escape this tangle,
I hoped, by cleaving to the placid Anglo,

The commonplaces of my mother's side,
Where all had noses of a decent size.

But they had spiked my blood and shaped my face,
The Oliveiras and Tavares. Late
In childhood, I began to feel my lips
Lift—with a fine, ironic, Latin twist—
At Anglo doings: Baptist-style communion,
With Wonder Bread and grape juice, sense of humor
Sparkling as bread, the pallid tendency
To slur their words on *beer* and fall asleep,
The milky food they boiled to blandness—decent,
Like their behavior, normal like their features.
Then in my teens it all began to show;
I watched my hair get dark and wavy, nose
And face get long; and sultry, shifty moods—
Endemic, I felt, to Portuguese— infused
The whole.

      But I had one more trick: the learning,
Loving, and making one with me of *German*
(Failing Norwegian, which they didn't teach).
Like the Germanic part of English—squeeze
The Latin out!—it seemed a crystal language,
My German, not a flow, all slurred and languid;
Clean as the angle-featured blonds who spoke it,
Who weren't unseemly, sweating, belching jokers.
English distilled, the anti-Portuguese,
Precise and clipped, not slushy! Leave the grease
To cousins—I'll be Raimund von Oliver,
Controlled and hard, beyond all squalid hurt.
The Anglo side triumphed like Sisyphus.
With words I made myself a German, pushed

Up to the summit of my Germanness . . .
I went to Germany, came home depressed.

Meanwhile, It had been waiting. Like a slosh
Of port across a linen tablecloth,
Making the white one red, indelibly,
My English fabric's drench of Portuguese,
Insistent now, was not to be denied,
Loud with the richness of its ruby dye.
For instance Uncle Tony. Welterweight,
And tough, he liked to jab them in the face,
No KOs, to enjoy them longer; taught me
To "use my hands"—good for a little softy
With hard potential. Wise guy, cheery giver
Of gifts, a lady's man, dangerous, vivid;
These virtues rhymed with my needs, as "Oliveira"
Fully rhymes with a bottle of madeira.

I started then to learn the language, eating
My *vinho-d'al's* and *caldo* and *linguiça*,
Mouthful by mouthful, foods and words, to build
My inner Portuguese, with taste, by will.

Unfair

I failed to weep
at my belov'ed mother's death because
she had been leaving us for years, bit
by bit, like a house she'd been moving
out of, chair by chair, book
by book. But when my father, who
had helplessly disliked me from the start,
suddenly died, I wept
like a child, he was so vivid,
funny, outrageous, right
down to his very hostility.
My mother earned the tears whose absence
she would have sweetly overlooked;
my father, who would have been
dumbfounded, got them.

Quite Distinctive

Among the bears and wolves and
bulls and prancing thoroughbreds
of Europe, Portugal
is a smiling cocker spaniel.
There's something of a bloodline running
through bloodless bullfights—
world's first country to stop
legally killing people—third
safest country of all,
these days:
the kind of place where
exquisite cubes of stone, each black
or white, are set in swirling curves
as sidewalks;
fine art OK
to walk on.

My Father Thinks of the Azores

At times, and suddenly, he had to eat
In old, passionate, earthy ways; no more
New England boiled dinner and sweets too sweet.
Then he would go to Whelan's, Yankee store,
But rich in fish so fresh in fine-hacked ice,
It smelled as clean as the sea; he bought as much
As needed for ancestral appetites,
Then stopped at Flory's bakery for such
Bread as the fish required, and hermits: thick,
Molasses-chewy, raisined, spicy slabs
To chase the serious stuff. He'd throw the slick
White paper packs of lobsters, codfish, crabs,
Or clams, or bleeding beef, or unctuous pork,
Across the table like a slap in the face
At puritans of food. With jabbing fork,
And slashing knife, he'd joyously unbrace
The pristine fish-flesh, toss it in the pot,
Or pan, or wetly slap a steak on the skillet;
While they boiled or sizzled, his stomach thought
On his behalf, daring the food to fill it.
At last, in noisy, wordless rapture, with each
Forkful of flesh or fish—the fat, the lean—
And chewy breads, his hungry will would reach
Back to the islands he had never seen,
To seize imagined hunks of heritage—
His by his language, loneliness, and rage.

Epilogue

Now it's all over: old and sick, all died.
First Mamie, loved by Manuel Reis, who played
At her wedding, then, rejected suitor, went
Down to the cellar where they found him later,
Broken guitar beside him, numbly soaking
His feet in a pail of water cold as failure.
She died all full of tubes, yellowed and smiling.
And Tony, whose pursuit of women drove him
From the Bucket of Blood in Charleston once,
Pursued by many sailors, who did not
Accept his touching, pressing need for women—
Tony repented of his need, both then
And when he jumped wailing into her grave,
Lily's, the wife he drove to suicide,
Some said. He died locked in his mindless head,
And moveless body, handsome as in youth.
And Father. Past his appetites, except
For laughter, still ironic but no longer
Powered and shaped by rage, he left in the night,
Without a word, as if the urgency
Of death embarrassed him. I'd wish him rest
From all his pained offenses. Oh, I wept.

That was all years ago. And now, as though
They were my characters that I created,
With setting, mood, and plot, they move about
In verse at my behest; so I forget

That I'm in part their character and child,
By genes and quirks of mind, but also words.
I speak a Portuguese, the sort you learn
From books and tapes—more than my fifty, sixty
Childhood words; their language, but on my terms.
I need to know the world through Portuguese,
So those adults, that child, and I, can speak.

AZORES, 1989

Terceira; São Miguel

The taxi like an open carriage rattled
Across the fields of soft cut hay to Angra,
Swirling our noses in the world of springtime,
Essence of hay for heads in jetlag, rinsing
The dregs of rancid sleep and sweat in sweetness,
Like inspiration.
      Later, in the haze
Rising where hot exhaustion meets a coldness—
Foreign surface—we saw a nonce hotel,
And in its bathroom found this sacrament,
This welcome: soap, *feno de Portugal*,
Its scent exact—the same hay we had breathed
Across the island, balm to flight-dried nostrils;
Minor olfactory echo; unexpected,
Endearing hint of Portuguese coherence.

The search for food led to a vaulted cellar,
Whose walls and wine and salty fish allowed
A settling in, a hunkering down of self.
I had been drifting in my rich dispersal,
So much of it, my head amazed with shifts
Of time and language, overload of senses,
The ringing, spinning impact of the real
On the imagined: Azores—fragile image,
For years; enchanted, far-off land I'd rigged
From anecdotes, the sea, a taste for yams;
And now this place, like any in its nowness.

25

We see the little city after supper,
Its people in the streets all evening . . . but
I want to save my living in the Azores
For São Miguel, ancestral best of islands.

Down like a hawk—*açor*—on São Miguel,
The airplane gently settles: Slender Point,
Ponta Delgada, biggest city, port
For most who come by sea, or, like my people,
Leave. In the early greyness trees are chirping
And wetly blooming; shyness getting slightly
Bolder as sunlight gropes through moving clouds.
Taxi, hotel. Amidst the practical,
I try, intent, to grasp a dream-born fact:
In ninety years, I'm the first of my line
Who's felt this island underfoot, and smelled it.
For good they left it. Am I one of them,
A compound self, a vessel for the dead
Whose minds have changed, and who've in time returned?
For that I'd need them (more than in my genes
And features) in my thoughts, and will, and feelings.
Then I could feel these splendid, cut-stone sidewalks,
Little cubes of white or black, alike,
Set as mosaic arabesques, or birds,
Or flowers—feel them not as exotica
But *sidewalk*, maybe with some local pride,
But mainly "something rain won't turn to mud."
But who can know the mind of long ago?
Maybe, as tourist of the generations,
I've come to see the inconceivable touch
Of time made touchable: the piling up
From stones to buildings, hamlets into cities,
The merely old becoming picturesque . . .

I'm visitor and witness. António,
If I am empathizing well with him,
Is maybe here with me; enhancing my stay.

How did I feel? The sky of clouds forever
Moving, greyish and whitish, pressed its mood
On humid air, fifties, sixties, and warming
To noon of white and blue, Portuguese colors;
And so I felt my soul was getting soaked,
Washed in the soft and rainy air by angels
Meaning me well, summoned by São Miguel.

Like Europe minor, businesslike yet easy,
A little charming, the cityscape repeats
The message of the heavens: nothing big,
Or loud, except hydrangeas crowding fences;
The trees all clipped, the streets all swept, the people
Keyed to a steady Latin pitch of chatter,
Hustling about among the glassy bars,
And shops, and coffeehouses—and many churches,
With scrolled façades and old, next to their towers
Full of bells not loud but mellow. Latin,
These people, but subdued, as if by coolness,
Greyness, and water. Many familiar faces,
Like uncles, cousins, none of whom I've met.
I'm half at home among the outsized noses
And ears, the skulls that jut way out in back,
Faces of longness often comical,
But somber; indoor skin with shoeblack hair.

And more than half dismayed. My hearing's bad;
The dialect is strange; I only get it
In bits. (But Mary Anne, my quick companion,

Who knows the language only through her Spanish,
Interprets; I reply in Portuguese,
Sounding as ever like a too-correct
Native from elsewhere; taken as a unit,
We're almost someone.) Azoreans distort;
They umlaut everywhere. *Dedos* is *döds,*
I am *Raimünd'*—Portuguese is enchanting,
Umlauts or not. Just take the names of towns:
Sintra, Cascais, Coimbra, Évora . . .
Like clarions far away, their hardness muted . . .
The language, though, is not a clarion
For me, but like a piano to be mastered.
Fradique Mendes, comic other voice
For Eça de Queiroz (it's odd how many
Gifted Portuguese need a double, or more—
Pessoa had a handful; are their lives
So rich they need to split for fear of bursting?)—
He says that languages are means, not ends:
"Tools for knowing, like tools for gardening.
Why work on grammar and a perfect accent?
That's like a gardener who carves the blade
And handle of his hoe with leaves and vines,
Playing with it instead of digging. How,
Then, would the planted vineyard grow, my friend?
Foreign languages should be mangled proudly."
True, a piano's not a tool for knowing,
So what to do but play it? But a language—
Ah, blesséd doubleness!—is best at both,
Playing and knowing. So excuse me, Eça-
Fradique; I will play your Portuguese.

* * *

I played the tourist too, and distant cousin,
Touring the quays where foreign freighters docked,
Feeling connected, telling anyone
I talked to my relation to the island,
Hoping, expecting I would be accepted—
As cousin? (Why this need? It's like a reaching
For membership in something everyone,
By right, belongs to.) Almost all responded,
Politely. But I got a sad comeuppance,
Twice. We were walking in a nicer quarter—
The trees were trimmed like poodles—when a beep
Made me look up. I waved with, as I thought,
Friendly response in kind, before I'd seen
The finger from the window, indicating:
Up Yours. The finger, gringo. Off he drove,
Pleased in his camionette; I stood there grieving,
Embarrassed at myself for smiling, waving,
Like almost one of them.
                              The other time
It was a crowded morning coffeehouse,
The kind with marble tables round and tiny.
I sat scrunching my face, absorbed in something—
Words, I suppose—and noticed two young men,
Three tables away; one was scrunching his face,
The other laughing. Pitiless mimicry!
Like looking in the mirror at a chimp.
I needed to be moving on from here.

We found the Archives. Entered in their records,
Remoter than the graves I looked for later,
I saw the faded traces of my family;
Their birth, not death—entered, not exited.

Rightful neglect of what was less important?
Important: they were born, had names, and worked
As *camponeses*—farming laborers.
But vital mostly were their names in Christ,
Handles for God to haul them out of death.

> *Their names, Francisco d'Oliveira*
> *And Margarida de Jesús,*
> *Exist in writing only here*
> *And there: a faint page in the Archives;*
> *Rainy stones in a place of weeds*
> *Behind a sea cliff in the Azores,*
> *The headstones slanting like the letters.*
> *Such little monuments in words!*
> *But maybe—Chico, Guida—for you*
> *Who could not write but hoped to be*
> *Written into the Book of Life,*
> *When all is finished, they will do.*

They had come from Pilar, Bretanha. So
We took the closest house on that same coast,
Rua dos Moinhos (Street of the Mills),
Mosteiros (Monasteries). These were gone,
But not the windmills—houses now—confronting
The North Atlantic still, as if the blowing,
Which almost never stops, could yet be made
To work. The blades, no longer milling grain,
Twirl in the wind as useless as the wind,
But with the harmonies of native art:

> *The walls of whitewash suit*
> *The salt of island air,*
> *And noon, and the blue glare*

Of sky; but mostly they suit
The surging windwash stress
Of windmill in the airswell—
White, in the colorless.

We often took the windmill walk. Our house,
Likewise off by itself and white, was less
Bare than barren in that relentless air;
A blank-faced bungalow of stucco, tile,
And glass; unlike the mills, it held no past.
Across the road the coast did not stretch out,
It seemed contracted to a sullen mass,
Its wild volcanic rock in crags, and boulders,
And crumblings, black like char in dirty ovens,
But ocean-cleaned. And over to our right,
Five hundred feet above the sea, atop
A massive cliff of black, sheer rock and sheer
Drop, was the village of Pilar—a spot,
Whitish. They were *camponeses* all right,
Vertically landlocked into tilling earth.
I'd try to find their vestiges and echoes.

For help we set out to the salty restaurant
Owned by our landlord, knower of his world.
Past greenish tidal pools that people used
For swimming; past the donkey carts that clattered—
Usefully, quaintly—through the town, on dirt
And cobbles; past the faces, old or vacant,
In windows open on the road, we walked
To early, oily dinner with Medeiros
And daughter; bought provisions; got directions.

We took a bus up to Pilar, and looked.
A minor village, tile and whitewashed plaster,
With spiky flowers in the tiny courtyards;
A plaza sparse with store, and bar, and church;
Some houses long abandoned, long collapsed.
I showed some people photos of Vovô.
Polite "ah, handsome man!" but no one knew,
Or even guessed at, cousins or descendants.
Gone like the smell of hay cut long ago.
Even the churchyard, locked, could not be seen;
I only glimpsed its graves, weedy and grey,
Through bars. We left the enclave of Pilar.

Family was me and some New England cousins.
The Azores part was over.
                              Had they stayed,
Who would I be? "*Je* est un autre" indeed:
"I" would be another, which has no meaning.
Meanwhile, and here, it's me—a tourist, but
One who must take this place as personally
As any praise or insult. "Azores" means . . .
Something of where I'm from. As if my hands,
And maybe stomach, had been made there, under
Local conditions, from the local clay.
My sense of humor (sharp, grotesque), the foods
I like and cook (spicy), accepting fate
(Mostly)—such things, Azorean, are mine,
Even perhaps a hands'-and-stomach's worth.
My father, formed by Portuguese, his first
Language, by all his people speaking, feeling
In it—*informed* like a porkchop by its sauce,
Taking on taste and color from the onions,

Tomatoes, garlic, sage—he formed some half
Of me, both taste and meat, habits and genes,
Until I more and more took over.
                                    Who
I am, is the question "Azores" partly answers.
Forebears—whether the kings of England or
The peasants of Pilar—give us direction,
Shape the course of the ball that fate is rolling.

Bilingual, Portuguese and English, half-breed:
This halfness is a doubleness, perhaps
Duplicity, that's balanced like my hands—
I'm ambidextrous—both together making
Their music. There are two of me. We speak
Complexly to each other, and to others.

My speaking/thinking/being Portuguese
Is entering my self extended: inward,
But outward, too, like going through a mirror
That takes me to the new, old world of Eça,
Camões, Antero, ships through freighted air,
Golden, spicy, vinous, empires ago.
I take to heart their pains and triumphs: Pedro
The Cruel forcing courtiers to kiss
The rotting corpse of his belovéd, propped up,
High on the throne—Inês de Castro (they
Had acquiesced in her assassination);
The dribbling deliquescence of the empire.
Triumph: the globe-encircling by Magellan,
Part of the trick that God had played—to give
"A little country to be born in, but
Th' entire world to die in" to these people.

So I approve, or not, of what they do.
It's like the doings of one's child, or parent.

* * *

We formed no friendships, met no family, left
No hearts behind, but lived a bit of life,
There in the Azores, shopping for the day
In little stores like forty years ago
At home; but finding pineapples and tea
As pungent local produce, fresh enough
To scent the kitchen—and brewed or bitten into,
Vivacity itself; maracujá,
In rum before our supper . . . This was translation
Of downhome everydayness into Azores.
A little after Holy Spirit Day—
Fireworks in the sky!—we left Mosteiros.

> *Tudo passa, tudo passará;*
> *Nada fica, nada ficará.*
> *Everything passes, everything will pass;*
> *Nothing remains, and nothing will remain.*

> *On Holy Spirit Day, they set the mass*
> *To fireworks to make the meaning plain*
> *Of this old song. Figures of smoke arise,*
> *Born of big bangs, and march along the air,*
> *Compact and upright. What a brave surprise*
> *They keep their forms so long, these forms we wear.*

* * *

They left an island for a continent,
Where going far was not opposed by ocean.
As doctor of the language they adopted,
I follow them easily, through air not seas;

34

After a restaurant meal of beef, in final
Extravagance of olive oil and salt;
The hyphenated native going home,
Luso-Americano, part with part.

HOMAGE TO GONÇALO MENDES

Gonçalo Mendes Ramires

I wish you well, Gonçalo Mendes, you
And Portugal. In vain I tried to break
The link between myself and "Portuguese,"
To make it like a glass of ruby port
As seen by some ferocious drunk—my father?—
After he'd sobered up ferociously
For good, the ruby having no more beauty,
Now, than a traffic light on STOP. But that
Was long ago, that ugly, puddled anguish,
Spreading out from a childhood best rewritten.
(And so, in time, I made myself a poet-
Translator, one whose writing is rewriting.)

Gonçalinho, in you I see myself—
Writ large and better, I confess; "confess,"
Since I've despised the easy finding of self
In others, like imagining my hands,
Now Horowitz's, playing Beethoven,
Beautiful brilliant thunder, skill and genius.
Easier than enhancing what one has.
But as my anguish sank in the ground of time,
The loathing of drink it had provoked went too;
Goblet in hand I stood up to my past,
Drank to its health, and threw off thankless pain.
My creaking doors opened to Portugal—
And in you walked, Gonçalo, slim and dapper,
Presenting me yourself as alter ego

So tactfully I had to take you on,
As if a Horowitz had deftly made
His hands my own. It only took a little,
A touch of your speech, its genial, sensitive,
Intense extravagance, and I'd been had
By kindness. You convinced me it was I
Who did the favor, taking in this strange
Figure out of a book, into my mind.
And meanwhile you allowed my self-ideal
To take its coloration from your self.
Sparrow, it turned flamingo—brown to pink,
And bigger, rising in the violet air,
To some apotheosis of the tropics.
We share a common nature, like that pair
Of birds (little enough). On that I built
A scheme to save the Portuguese in me.

I've had to know you well to think you wholly.
And there you are: affable, svelte, and fair,
Of well-kept whiteness like a porcelain figure;
With fine and smiling, easily gentle eyes,
A moustache light and curly brown, Vandyke
Beard to elongate your already long,
Distinguished face; forever elegant,
And neat, in formal suit and polished shoes . . .
I am like you in hints and glimpses, mostly;
In general shape and hues; in pleasures shared,
Like mocking human folly, and extremeness
Of speech—enough to let me seize the day,
Your eighteen ninety-six, and make it mine.
I need to do that to imagine how
My Portugueseness might be likeable.

Delightful, even. We will see, Gonçalo.
I need to think about your life, and speak
With you.
      Now let us look to these adventures
You made of your mostly quiet, happy days.

Dinner at Gago's

You never took your food or drink for granted.
Even a whiff of tea and toast expanded
Your mood and nostrils; and the thought of *feasting*
Moved you to Rabelaisian gestures, speeches,
Every extravagance. Was it the whole
Process you found so droll—sublimely gross?
This in-at-the-mouth, out-at-the-fundament,
Triumph and joy (at best) at either end,
Spirit and body, dual human nature?
The secret shame of food! Regurgitated,
Who would eat it again? Yet that same mess,
Moments before, had been our pleasure, pressed
Against our palate, secretly delicious.
Yes, you would see in this our health and sickness:
Such privacy is isolation—yet
How lovely the regaling in our head.

In part, your foodness must have been ancestral,
From him of sub- or superhuman, bestial
Or godlike appetite, that old Ramires
That Castanheiro praised for vital, fearless,
Heroic strength; a man equipped to eat
A pair of suckling pigs at a Christmas feast
("Only a belly he was, but what a belly!
I see him, porkified and supine, swelling
With the unconscious greatness of your race—
Caramba what a man! Enough to make

Tears of tenderness soak my beard"). Imagine—
To move the bowels of Portuguese compassion
By eating a pair of pigs. Your heritage,
Gonçalo: viva the alimentary tract!

But you have made things sociable, refined,
Verbal, though still voracious, like that time
In Vila Clara, ten o'clock one night
In summer by the fountain. Cool despite
The lingering heat, your cronies sat and waited,
Fanning themselves; at last, in the elation
Of need you came, announcing "serious,
Historic, monstrous hunger of Ramires,"
Allowing no delay for getting brandy,
"To Gago's! Gago's! There's no time! I'm famished
With this immense Ramiric hunger! Move!
Or I'll have to cut a chop from one of you!"
And off you hopped like Monty Python's knight,
Your hands together, neighing, making like
Both horse and rider, with your little rabble,
Galloping headlong to your favorite tavern.

And in the lofty room above the bar,
Up steep and narrow stairs, now taking charge
Of merrymaking at the table (handsome,
Long, and lit by a chandelier with candles),
You shouted that by miracle your sickness—
Indigestion—was cured, "as God's my witness,"
And to prove it you ate a crowded plate
Of eggs and sausage, gobbled half a plaice,
A "sick man's chicken," cucumber salad bathed
In oil, and slabs of bread and marmalade.

At last, you had poor weary Gago making
"Tremendous coffee! Strong enough to waken
Talent in Senhor Barros!" Then cigars,
And Videirinha playing his guitar.
(All this, with pints of wine, and yet your pale,
Delicate skin was not a bit enflamed.)

That's how I want to live. It's like the feast
In heaven: earthiness sublime, and free
Of deep-set flaws embedded in our earth,
Like boredom, fear, depression, hate, and worse.
You found it funny, fundamental, lively
To be embodied; public farce, yet private
(And harmonized as if by Mozart) pleasure,
Through talking, laughing, drinking, eating together.

The Tower, Santa Ireneia

Veranda, dining room, and library
Are where you live, at home in soul and body,
Since in all three you read and write and eat—
Your pleasing trinity of *summum bonum*.
I've tried, in kitchen, yard, and living room,
To do the same, in my American way,
Which is to yours as sprawling is to sitting.
Two kinds of *bonum*: mine's the lesser, yours
The older, richer, therefore larger. Not stiff,
But formal even when at ease, you show
The Way, this Sunday late in June, absorbing
The heat and silence of afternoon, enacting
La Dolce Vita—for you, *A Doce Vida*.
(A heritage like long features, and blondness,
This place has likewise made Gonçalo Mendes,
Bequeathing all the means, and nuanced values,
By which to take his ease, that is, to live.)

Library first, your sometime place of work:
It's large and light, with plastered walls of azure
To match the sky, but heavy ebony
For bookcases—the places of repose,
In dust, of folios with calfskin covers,
Theology and law, ancient and thick.
A blend of quintessential in- and outdoors,
It breathes by two windows that give a view
Of lemon-orchards, and allow their scent

To grace the indoor weightiness. The windows,
With sill and seat of stone, and velvet pillows,
Are open to your cool, covered veranda,
Where honeysuckle rambles up the railings.
Your kind of beauty: old, yet new with freshness.
And at these windows facing the veranda—
And vast, with sun-discolored covering
(A crimson damask), and the piled-up works
Of Scott, and genealogy, with two
Vases of pink carnations—your table waits.
There you can sit in vivid sunlight, breathing
A mixed bouquet of leather, paper, flowers,
And tea and toast, and lemon trees—and work.
That is your genius: everything together.

* * *

Your dining room, which faces that veranda
Through doors of glass, is where you gather cronies
For tasteful dinners served from the buffet—
Marbled sideboard of dark mahogany—
On dishes from Japan, with family silver.
But lunch and breakfast, summers at least, you take
On that refreshing, luminous veranda,
Reminded of your family past by finest,
Eighteenth-century glazed and blue-white tiles
To midpoint up the wall, and, in the corner,
A soft, deep sofa, damask-rich, for smoking.
Here you can contemplate your whole estate,
Along the river to Valverde Hills.

You cannot see me, Gonçalinho, looking
Back from a century ahead, enjoying

Your life as you enjoy it, I imagine.
Not for your wealth and leisure, pleasing manners,
Refined intelligence, and kindliness,
But for precisely your delight in living—
Just in the way you do, which lets you savor
The common, heady freshness of the air,
On the veranda early, and the sun,
Just up, already blazing, bringing fragrance
Of lemon as you take a light collation,
Your toast and tea, and read that verse romance
By Uncle Duarte, and start to write your novel,
Happily broken in on by Titó,
Who needs your camaraderie and tea.
You savor each of these events, and all
Together, not as prefaces to something—
Your day, your life—but as that life itself,
As such; *it never will be more or better.*
And that's a truth we've mastered, you and I.

Ana Lucena, Rosa de Rio Manso, and Friends

You had enjoyed the otherness of women,
Amicably, as both a gift and given.
But Dona Ana: you were drawn to her
As to a source of heat. But, oh, she purred
Fatly, as though a mango, overripe,
Had learned to talk. And used correct, polite
Address—"Of course the Cavalier may smoke"—
You found absurd. But you had tasty hopes,
Excited when her sick, rich husband died;
And she had black, refulgent, liquid eyes,
Ripe lips, white teeth, and tight beneath her dress,
You gathered, graceful limbs and perfect breasts.
"But she's a butcher's daughter; you'd expect
Just what she is—a splendid piece of flesh.
But common; not a crumb of grace or soul.
And Jesus, what a voice! And what a bore."

You thought her lacking, then, but practical:
"I find this person excellently dull,
Like some tomato ripe to pluck and eat.
And I'm a *tasteful* connoisseur—though pleased
With such exuberance of womanhood,
Not moved to penetrate beyond her looks
Into an inwardness that must delight me
As would the mind of a marble Aphrodite."

Intimacy with Ana could be deep
In inches only, so you had to see

Where she had been: *what was her reputation?*
I see in this how clearly we're related.
We might discount a husband foolish, ancient,
Doubtless impotent, like her limp Lucena;
But others? Ravenous affairs in Lisbon?
For other men to be in a position
To say, "I know your wife as well as you,
Bodily," and to back this claim with truth,
With infamous, lascivious detail—
This, to our pride, is *lèse majesté*,
A flaying of our sacred privacy.
"Her breasts? I know exactly how they feel,
How they respond." And all lovers could say
That much and worse. Jealousy, shame, and rage!
Would be our itching, biting bedmates then.
We'll have no retroactive cuckoldry!

And so your closest friend, Titó, aware
Of your predicament, said "You can't marry
This woman. I don't know, in all, how many,
But she has had at least one lover. Ask
No questions. That's enough about her past.
It's I who tell you; and I never lie."

You said goodbye to money, liquid eyes,
And succulent flesh.
           At length you found your virgin,
Rozinha, budding last you'd seen her, coming
To flower fully now, blushing and lovely,
Viscount of Rio Manso's daughter, public
And private prize eleven years your junior.
What of intelligence and sense of humor?
I'd need them in my virgin; you, perhaps,

Had found that anything but beauty distracts
(Assuming family, youth, and wealth, you'd say)
From femaleness, which must be taken straight,
Like brandy. For the rest, you may depend
On Vilalobos, on Titó—on friends.

How Gonçalo Became a Local Saint

Once, on the hill above Corinde, Gonçalo
Noticed a hot commotion down below,
And stopped his horse to watch: some carts and wagons,
People on foot or mule, a bright confusion,
With yells and gestures—then dispersal, sudden,
The woman trotting off on her mule, the others
Jolting and squeaking through the dust on wheels;
All but one man, his jacket on his shoulder,
Who limped with painful slowness down the road.
Gonçalo thought this odd, and went to see.
The man, his leg all shrunken, raised a face
Wrinkled in pain and glistening with liquid,
Like a decaying pear, and painfully,
Politely told the story of his ankle.

"A running sore for months. Nothing can dry it,
Not plasters, myrtle dust, or even magic.
Was on the way to Senhor Julio's place,
Slipped on the path, a rock fell down and hit it,
Opened it even more and cracked the bone,
Left it like this. I had to rip my shirt up
To sop the blood—now watch it soaking through!"

This laborer, one Manuel Solha, came
From Finta; had to walk the whole way back.

"You can't! Couldn't you get some help? Those people,
With horses, carts?" "Not in this world, my Lord,
They're all too busy. But that girl, she lives
In Finta . . . maybe send some help . . ." And Solha,
Panting, smiling, winced as his ankle twisted,
When he tried to steady the leg. At once,
Gonçalo lightly dismounted: "Fine, then, horse
For horse; take this one." Solha gaped at him.
"What? By the holy name of God! I go
On horseback, and your lordship goes on foot?"
Gonçalo laughed: "Man, with this talk of 'me
On horseback, you on foot,' we're losing time!
Now just be quick, get on, and ride to Finta."
The other, shaking his head and shuddering,
As if at sacrilege, moved back a step:
"Certainly not, my lord, certainly not!
I'd rather die right here—and gather mold
On the wound!" Gonçalo stamped his foot, commanding,
"Get up, I order you! You work the fields,
Work with a hoe, I've got a doctor's degree,
Coimbra, I'm the one who knows, it's me
Who gives the orders!" So, submissively,
The peasant slipped his good foot in the stirrup,
Aided by the aristocrat, who didn't
Remove his white gloves to avoid the blood,
And off they went together side by side.

"But this is the End of Time!—here am I,
On Lord Ramires's horse, and there's the lord,
Senhor Gonçalo Mendes Ramires da Torre,
On foot beside me, going down the road!"

A certain kind of time, Gonçalo, yes,
Had ended: the millennium of perfect
Aristocratic arrogance unquestioned,
Relieved by little deeds of mercy merely
For getting into heaven; like a feast—
A sloshing, gut-busting, colossal orgy—
Followed by alms of garbage for the poor,
Leftovers crammed in baskets, dumped at the gate.
But you, intelligent in tenderness,
Corrected that millennium by using
Its arrogance for mercy, like a surgeon
Who hurts our flesh to get at cancer: hoping
To save his body in the only way
You knew would work, you pressed that peasant's will
Down with your own, in tenderest oppression.

And everybody knew, and you were sainted,
As better than the Good Samaritan,
Because, a noble, you had bent much lower
In your *beau geste*—superb *noblesse oblige!*
I know your secret, though: you had no thoughts
Of gesture, obligation, or effect,
You suffered with that suffering and simply,
Quickly, did what you could, as if by reflex.
(I saw it, too, in your pain, when Cavaleiro
Kept that poor man waiting; and in the way
You had compassion for Casco's little son.)
Simplicity of heart—not principles,
Or theories—shapes your charity, and makes it
Fresh as spearmint, not big, official, godly.
Me too: I want to be, in this, like you.

History

One is already something, as *Gonçalo*
Mendes Ramires. One is meant to follow
The vector of the past, which, like a ray
Of sun- or moonlight, or a comet's tail,
Is long and bright. Not like a falling rock,
Natural model for the common lot,
The others. History is for you a pageant,
Where one of you has always been an actor,
As if one big Ramiric character,
Shared by different bodies, were always heard,
Shouting the family motto, differently
Inflected, down the last ten centuries.
You were among the vague, remote Senhores
Maintaining castles between Minho and Douro
Against the Franks; and at Ouriques a vision,
Above the battle, of the crucifixion,
Came to you on a cloud of gold; Tavira,
Alcácer Quibir, Aljubarotta, Arzila—
You were there, with your sword or broadaxe swinging,
Your name and valor older than the kingdom.

And now before you stands the ancient tower.
As remnant and reminder, it empowers
Your literary grasp of who you are,
Its foursquare blackness like a solemn charge:
"Remember, reimagine these thousand years—

They finally lead to you, Mendes Ramires!"
The Tower of Dom Ramires, as you called it,
Was your response, a tale of old, appalling
Vengeance ("horrors," you said), the style heroic,
Stately, of one whose enemy was slowly,
In terror, sipped to death by giant leeches—
Lashed naked to a stake in a pond, and reaching
In vain for water as he died of thirst.
Such family stories ("we were killers") hurt,
But bound you to the land, made you at home
In history; you would never feel alone.
With art, you "carried the tradition on,"
As Castanheiro urged; your own, and long,
It comes to lurid ripeness in your words,
Which make poetic sense of the absurd:
Those actions of your monstrous Tructesindo,
Who models vengeance, pride, and rage obscenely.
Though family, you present him in the best
Portuguese mocking way, as a burlesque
Of brainless heroism—which we notice
Only later, you're such an artful joker.

* * *

An Oliveira isn't "something," isn't
"Already"; he's an unknown, not a given.
Ours is a trail of one who walked through grass,
Dropping faint bits of paper as he passed.
No tales of flashy deeds, no monuments
As remnant and reminder; just the bent
Grass and some recollections, late and small;
We're free from history as if not involved . . .

History's a box of wonders for the choosing,
Not an exacting record of the doings
Of one's protracted self. I seek out real
Meetings with *any* place, in books I read—
With Faulkner's Mississippi, Hawthorne's New England . . .
I strive to meet Magellan, say, by thinking
His ship, with probables and constants: groaning,
Creaking wood under stress; a dizzy rolling,
Slightly checked by the keel; the stinks; the greasy
Feel of pork not salted enough, with weevils;
And constants, like the sun and wind and sea.
So for a moment live as touch, I meet
Magellan as though no time had come between us
Dense as a mountain; suddenly there's meaning,
Flaring and fading; I am in that past.
And this "historical sensation" casts
A long, warm afterglow.
                    So after all,
Gonçalo, I too make history *personal.*

Homage to Gonçalo Mendes

You are a man of senses, if not sense
In all respects, and, being Portuguese
(As Senhor Maia says, who knows the whys
And hows of that condition), cannot be
A lover of ideas; what you love,
Hotly, is form; your mania for making,
Then playing with a handsome phrase—absorbed,
Enchanted with its music—always wins.
Let thought go down the drain, but save the language!
And other beauty moves you: every shading
Of glass and wood and leather at the Tower;
The foods and wines that wet both mouth and eyes;
The moon-clear music of your troubadour,
The soothing Videirinha; Ana's fruitlike,
Fresh-ripe surface you love as such; a ride
On horseback, on a sweetly misty Sunday;
September's air, becalmed, and clear except
For smoke from fireplaces, light and slow . . .

But then we see the worms, when Lady World
(Resplendent front! arousing all our senses)
Shows us her back—a mass of putrid ooze,
A corpse with squirming life, the other side
Of our obsession with the sensuous.
I think of how they made their kings—embalmed
Badly—a public show, discolored ears

Or noses crumbling damply. How they love
Our flesh alive or dead, with joy or terror!

So when you showed the family crypt, you joked
With Cousin Maria, eager Ramiphile,
And spoke a final truth for both of us:
"Ancestors! Just a bit of worthless dust.
Right, Dona Ana? Really, who'd conceive
That Cousin Maria here, so lovely, so
Alive, so sweetly pert, could be descended
From such a pinch of dust, kept in a trough
Of stone? It can't be done, oh no! You can't
Link so much life to so much nothingness."
The discontinuity is absolute;
Those men of force and pride indeed descended
To nameless, nearly weightless earth, or bones.
They did; and when my mind is touched by this,
The Gorgon-thought, it stops. And then the thought
Loosens, Gonçalo, and we move, but not
To grasp it, like a wrestler with a slackened
Opponent; we move on, to vanity—
Of every human endeavor, mainly ours,
Like your discreet political ambition,
Or the poetic one I'd kept for years.
(That day you got elected deputy,
They fêted you; and then the fireworks,
Depleted, left a night serenely black.)
You saw the people loved you after all,
That day; they shouted, waved, and laughed with you.
You'd won: Lord of the Tower but humble, saintly,
St. Martin sharing not his cloak but horse.
(But you would not have cut a horse in two,

Even to help a bleeding peasant!) Yet
You knew in triumph, too, that vanity
Prevailed. You hadn't needed Cavaleiro—
Local Don Juan, connected politico;
And yet to win you'd pimped for him your sister
(Sad in her marriage to a fat buffoon),
Telling yourself that it was all for friendship.
Your putting him again in touch with Graça,
Who loved him still though he had jilted her—
Your letting *that* one dine at your table!—led
Straight to the sunroom, words you overheard,
And acts you shuddered at: "No, no, what madness!"
"Yes, yes, my love!" You sorrowed much, and long.

Not merely saint, but hero to the people!
A true Ramires from the brutal, brilliant
Past! To yourself, for years, a rabbit; then
You roared.
                    Your flesh and senses would betray you,
You always said; if danger came you fled,
Or went all queasy in the stomach pit.
I know this too. It isn't fear of losing
A fight, it's knowing what your frightful honor
Demands: to crush the insult absolutely.
And that could mean disfigurement—your teeth
Knocked out, a broken nose, all kinds of pain;
Radical torment to the man of senses,
Whose vanity's as fragile as his nerves.
And unlike me, you as Ramires must
Endure the gaze of heroes down the ages . . .
They saw you flee from Casco on the road,
Then twice, and almost thrice, from that Ernesto,

The bully from Nacejas, woman chaser,
Braggart, who just for fun reviled, and mocked,
And jeered at you—much your superior
In strength, and endlessly in self-assertion.
The third time, though. He'd stopped you on the road,
Laughing, with club in hand: "Going somewhere,
Ramires-shit?" And then a mist confused
Your eyes. A howl rose from your total being,
Your jerked the reins in a surge of pride, and fury,
And force, it made your horse rear like a tower,
The bully grabbed the reins, you stood up high
On stirrups, brought your vicious three-edged whip
Whistling down on his face, ripping an ear
In two, down on his mouth, scattering teeth . . .
The bully lived; for which, when you regained
Awareness, you were thankful. But you thanked
Much more the fate that made you a Ramires—
Fully, at last—to neighbors, yourself, and past
Ramires men. They smile; you're one of them.

It was a *word* that freed Ramires-power
In you, as if a spell had been undone.
You've always lived in words, and in your senses,
Which you enhance by fusing them with words,
As words in turn catch light if set to verse.
And your extravaganzas with the language!
Irony glinting like an ice storm, changing
The world; your metaphors grotesque as gargoyles;
Joking, invective, parody, affection—
You wielded Portuguese like Toscanini
Conducting. That was in lieu of being cruel,
Physically, thus a hero—true Ramires.

But when you heard that curse that fouled your name,
You rose up and became a hero too.

So words create the world, Gonçalo, yours
And mine at least. What's "Portuguese" to me?
Yes, family—father, Tony, Vovô, people,
The Azores—and the language, and some books.
Family was often painful, Azores distant.
What I accept, delight in, love as mine,
Is feeling Portuguese in mouth and mind.
It scents the mind it fills, as *madressilva*,
In vases, makes a room its own completely,
Pungently; and I love what it achieves
With style, as shown in verse and choicest prose,
None choicer than your own, Queiroz; but mostly,
I love this world you made, Gonçalo, Eça,
A Portugal benign, absorbing, comic,
A mess at business, timid but heroic,
Primping and vain but deep and simple-hearted,
Practical yet fantastic . . . it is you,
Gonçalo, who are Portugal—and you
Who stepped up as my godfather, and let
My sour Portuguese grapes become a port
Of sweetest, richest vintage; you, this mellow
World that consists of words of Portuguese.